I KNOW WHERE MY FOOD GOES

JACQUI MAYNARD

illustrated by

KATHARINE MCEWEN

© 2001 LeapFrog Enterprises, Inc.
I KNOW WHERE MY FOOD GOES written by Jacqui Maynard; Text © 1998 Walker Books Ltd.
Illustrations © 1998 Katharine McEwen. Reproduced by permission of Walker Books Ltd., London.
Published by Candlewick Press, Inc. Cambridge, MA. All rights reserved.

Sam charged into the kitchen. "What's for lunch, Mom? I'm starving!"

"Hmm...let's see," said Mom. "Stewed slugs? A nice plate of grilled worms in mud sauce?"

"I know," she said. "How about pizza, with strawberry ice cream for dessert?"

Sam grinned. "YUM! My mouth's watering!"

"That's because it's getting ready to eat something," said Mom. "Set the table for me, will you, Sam?"

Sam got out some knives and forks. "Yeah," he said, "I know all about that. The watery stuff's called sal...sal...something."

"**Saliva**," said Mom. "Your body makes about 1½ quarts of it every day —that's almost the same as eight glasses of milk!"

"Oh, right," said Sam. "But I know what **saliva** does. It makes food go all squishy so I can swallow it!"

MOUTH

Saliva

GO

"That's right," agreed Mom. "And what else should you do before you swallow food?"

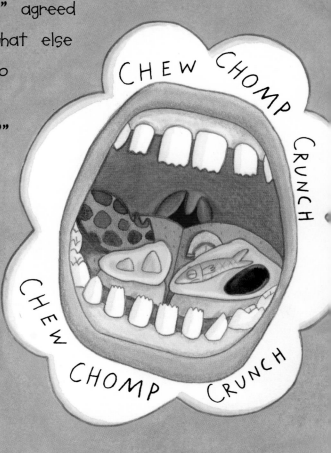

"**CHEW** it and **CHOMP** it and **CRUNCH** it all up," shouted Sam.

STOP

6

"And when it's all soft and slimy, I swallow it, and it goes all the way down the food tube from my **mouth** to my **stomach!**"

"Right again," said Mom, handing Sam some plates. "The food tube is called an **esophagus**, and lots of other animals have them, too. Cats and dogs have an **esophagus**, for example, and so do birds."

"Do they?" asked Sam. "Even birds like ostriches?"

"Yes," said Mom.

Sam laughed. "I bet an ostrich has a long **esophagus**!"

"I bet it has," said Mom, "and a really skinny one, too. Yours is about half as long as your arm, and only as wide as your thumb!"

9

GO

"And guess what," she said, as she put the pizza in the oven, "even if you're standing on your head, your food still goes straight to your **stomach**. Don't try eating upside down though, or you might choke!"

"Course I won't," said Sam. "But does it really?"

STOP

"Yes, really," said Mom. "The food doesn't just slide down your **esophagus**. The muscles inside it squeeze the food along, just the way you squeeze toothpaste out of a tube."

"Oh," said Sam. "Okay."

"But I know what happens next," Sam said, putting two glasses on the table. "My **stomach** is like a big stretchy bag. And it squishes and squashes the food around and around until it's all gloopy and gloppy, like soup."

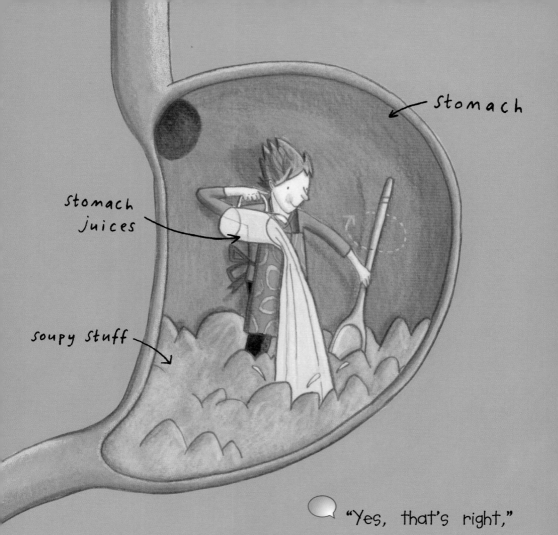

stomach

stomach juices

soupy stuff

 "Yes, that's right," said Mom. "And while the food's in your **stomach**, it's churned around and around with a watery mixture called the **stomach juices**. They help turn the food into soupy stuff."

"Yeah," said Sam, "that's what I'm saying. And..."

"AND if you swallow lots of air or fizzy drinks with your food," said Mom, filling up the water pitcher, "you get air in your **stomach**. And sometimes the air comes rushing back up again, and you..."

GO

STOP

"BURP!" yelled Sam.
"We have burping contests
at school."

"Oh, you do?" said Mom.
"Well that's why we're not
having fizzy drinks!"
And she put the water
pitcher down on
the table.

STOP

"Anyway, I wasn't going to tell you about the burping," said Sam, huffily. "I was going to tell you what happens next.

What happens next is the soupy stuff squirts out of my stomach into another tube."

"That's right," said Mom. "There's a special muscle at the bottom of your stomach that works like a faucet. It lets the soupy stuff out a little at a time."

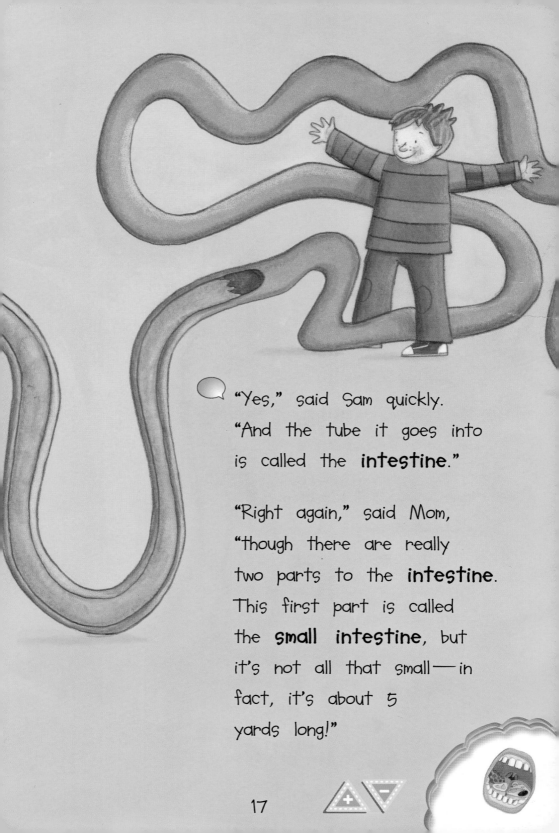

"Yes," said Sam quickly. "And the tube it goes into is called the **intestine**."

"Right again," said Mom, "though there are really two parts to the **intestine**. This first part is called the **small intestine**, but it's not all that small—in fact, it's about 5 yards long!"

"WOW!" said Sam. "That's about as long as...as..."

"Hmmm," said Mom, thinking about it. "I don't know what it's as long as either, but it's about as tall as a giraffe. And it's all folded up like spaghetti in a bowl, so it fits inside you."

"The **small intestine** is where all the good things in the soupy stuff get taken into your body," explained Mom.

"That's what **digestion** is," she added, putting a big bowl of salad on the table. "It's the way your body breaks down food and takes the goodness out of it, to give you energy and help you grow."

Sam sighed. "And that's why you're always saying green stuff like spinach is good for me," he said. **"YUCK!** I hate spinach! It's all slippery and slimy and it tastes like..."

Yuck!

"Yes, yes, all right," said Mom, opening the oven door. "But vegetables really are good for you—they have **vitamins** in them, and you need **vitamins** to keep you strong and healthy."

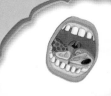

"I know, I know!" Sam sat down at the table. "But I know something else that happens in my **intestine**," and he giggled. "There's gassy stuff in it, too, isn't there? 'Cause that's why I pass gas."

"Well, yes, there is," said Mom. "The gas comes from the bits of food that aren't used up in your **small intestine**."

"See," he said, "I told you I
knew all about it, didn't I!"

Can I eat
my pizza now?